# IN BLUE MOUNTAIN DUSK

# IN BLUE MOUNTAIN DUSK

POEMS BY

## TIM MCNULTY

Broken Moon Press ○ Seattle

Some of these poems were first published in the following publications:
*Ark, The Bellingham Review, The Bloomsbury Review, Chelsea,
Columbia, Communique, Contact II, Coyote's Journal, Crab Creek
Review, Dalmo'ma, Duckabush Journal, Dream Network Journal,
Hanging Loose, Jeopardy, Kah Tai Anthology, Longhouse, Malahat
Review, Midnight Lamp, New Oregon Review, Not Man Apart, Outdoors
West, Poetry Now, River Styx, Seattle Review, Spoor, Voice of the Wild
Olympics, We'll Be Here a While Yet, Whole Earth Review, Willow
Springs, Yakima,* and in *Tundra Songs* (Empty Bowl Press), *Last Year's
Poverty* (Brooding Heron Press), *As a Heron Unsettles a Shallow Pool*
(Exiled-in-America Press), *Rain in the Forest, Light in the Trees:
Contemporary Poetry of the Northwest* (Owl Creek Press), *Wilderness
Scenario* (American Geographic Series), "Transition" broadside
series (Brooding Heron Press), and *At the Foot of Denali*
(Copper Canyon Press).

Printed in the United States of America.

ISBN 0-913089-32-x
Library of Congress Catalog Card Number: 92-70011

Broken Moon Press
Post Office Box 24585
Seattle, Washington 98124-0585 USA

For Mary

## [ I ]

# FROM THE CORDILLERA

## [ II ]

# GEESE AND REEDS

## [III]
## TUNDRA SONGS

# [IV]
## LAST YEAR'S POVERTY

# [V]
## THE STONE OWL

*He wouldn't answer*
*but followed the last light*
*up a steep broken ridge,*

*a cloth shirt and not*
*water enough for a cup*
*of broth.*

*From a shadowed meadow,*
*I watch him disappear*
*among boulders, too far*

*to hear my shout*
*and too late to make it*
*back by dark.*

*Nothing, now, but to follow*
*in blue mountain dusk*
*those heedless tracks across a snowfield,*

*the blind vision leading*
*headlong toward some fall*
*or ascendance.*

# [ I ]
## FROM THE CORDILLERA

# Spring and the River's Answer

### 1

Dusk and the old trees stir
on the far bank,
a warbler
trills across the springthaw torrent,
soft winds
preen in the bankgrass.

### 2

Down from the chill snowy pass
my friends
have followed out to the road,
voices ebb
at the edge of a clearing,
move off soft
as deer.

### 3

And those same thoughts that
drew me away—
once here
have slipped like thin papery husks
at the tips of branches
at budburst.

# Little River Love Poem

The early summer light
steps birdlike
down the east slope of Green Mountain
and stirs low mists along the river
into flight.

Back inside, you lie
still asleep in your summer skin.
A blue sheet thrown back like a dress,
your dark hair
spilled rain over your shoulders.

Having so much and nothing at all
to say,
I slip cold arms around you.
You turn, sleepily,
and a deep green river
drifts away in your waking eyes.

From a wooden skiff
tied to a salmonberry bush,
you step ashore,
holding in your arms
everything I ever let slip away.

# Currant Blossom Poem

for Jody Aliesan

Because they've just opened their eyes,
I'm careful to step around the small violets.
And because the trillium haven't yet come
to bloom, I look closely—arms
piled up with wood.

Because green, the winter's wood
must be felled in spring.
Wheelbarrow, split and stack to season,
when the redwings come glinting back
and geese clatter north through morning fog.

Twelve ricks to fill the shed,
two cord rounds; more green to mix in fall.
Whose fall?

Because the rain is sweet with pollen
and the creeks are up,
(even though the land's been sold)
"hauling water, chopping wood"
when the wild currant blooms in the creek!

# With the Moon

Barely free of the branches
        Leo
   dips a paw.

The tide thunders in at midnight
   quiets & moonweary creeps
            away.

We lay more driftwood
        over the coals,
lean back with a fresh pot of tea.

A doe
   pads the softwashed sand,
dawn moves lazily down.

        Damp clothes, empty bowls,
   Issa & sake,
           the morning star;
day,
       a small boat filled with light,
         is poised on an offshore swell.

# Typing a Poem for a Friend,
# I Stop and Listen to a Woodpecker
# Accompanying Me from a Snag
# Across the Creek

after James Wright

The deep hollow knocks carry through the trees,
Down the quiet mumble of the creek
And weave their way into the small racket of my typing.
I stop.
The random pauses and flurries, the single drawn notes seem
So much sweeter than mine. Inspired,
I haul the old machine out onto the roof.
The morning is cold and white with frost; the sun
    has not yet broken past the trees.
In a long liquid pause, I close my eyes and begin
    hitting keys, haphazard, hoping to maybe match
    its rhythms; I've always
Longed to talk to woodpeckers this way.
A single winter wren flutters up to the edge of the roof,
And the world is suddenly filled with light.

# In Their Time

for Nicholas Pearson

I like to be there—
late spring at the far reaches of treeline—
when the mountain hemlock and subalpine fir
first break out of the deep snowpack:
soft-sliding blanket that had laid them
bough and stem to the slope
while the weight of winter moved past.

It's the warmth of the life in these small trees
slowly melts through the frozen grip,
and on a day of sun-loosened crust,
a break-through-to-your-knees day full of juncos
and the skittery tracks of marmot,
they will upturn like a drawn bow
and with a sudden springing burst of snow
right themselves once more into treehood.

I like to think of the one winter
when each of them, thickened with the years
of snowmelt and wind,
find that singular strength to hold straight
through the deepening snows;
to have turned the great bows of their trunks
into the slope, and held there;
lifting, finally
out of the slow dance of the years
as all things lift in their time.

# Autumn Equinox

for Mary

Above the river, high
on a springy limb,
a squirrel is cutting green cones
and hard little *thunks* echo
       through the trees.

It's Equinox, our anniversary,
and again I'm working away from home.
Late morning, sunny,
not cold but not quite warm
as I shape a fir log for a bridge stringer
five miles up the Soleduck trail.

Rough bark curls over the drawknife,
white chips jump from the axe-bit
and tumble down the hillside,
while a soft rain of straw-dry needles
filters through long shafts of light.

The second year now I've been off
working on this day—midpoint
in the year's turn
     when we chose to marry—
the same slant of light through the trees.

Away from you now,
the old tastes and measures of a life alone
mean nothing to me;

as beneath my hands, the hidden,
deep-grained and polished heart
of a man and woman's life together
      emerges
   like newly shaped wood,

to bridge a way over this time away,
and keep us one.

# The Wind in Lost Basin

for Pat and Tina O'Hara

All night long
the wind honed the slate
and sandstone boulders—a late
September wind,
just beginning to cut its teeth.

It whittled at the talused ridge,
moaned softly in the spindled trees,
rattled the slender seed stalks
to their knees.

All the flapping tentfly night—
like wind in the sails of a small lost boat,
a ruffle
in the marmot's thickening coat,
sheen of ice in the shallows
that one day soon won't melt away,
the balance tipped to dark
from day.

No moon.
Arcturus low,
and the Hunter slowly picking his way
up the glacier.

# The Fog in Leland Valley

On autumn nights
when low fog drifts in
over Leland Valley,
the old cedar fenceposts
begin to take root.

I see them often,
driving home late in smoky moonlight,
         my lights off . . .

They lean this way or that
out of the low curls
           of groundcloud,
and once, weaving
I admit a little tipsily,
saw one lift tentative shoots of mist
into the secret light.

No one knows this.
By day
they slip back into fencelines—
     slack strands of rusty wire,
     lichen-feathered posts
           capped with moss—
only the roots stay.

It's the fog puts them up to it.
Fog
remembers when long ago
the valleys were deep with spruce and cedar,
and swamps were everywhere.

Fog misses that.

Now,
when barn owls
swoop the roadside draws
and the cows all huddle close,
I steer with both hands,
carefully through the slow spreading arms
of fog, the dark shapes of trees,
the bats;
while the old cedar posts drift by
wrapped in their dreams like stones.

# Poem to Rid the Woods of Jeremiah's Monsters

Because you see monsters
most everywhere these days,
and today on the path out from the cabin,
had to carry big sticks
to fight them,
and cried when the weight slowed you down.

And even though I haven't seen them,
I know they're there, too.
So I make this poem
to rid the woods of monsters.

All you monster eyes
that see only to ravage the poor and voiceless
of the world,
    *Go blind!*

Hands that snatch the very ground
from beneath unborn feet,
    *Go limp!*

Teeth that tear at the last thin shreds
of what is green and holy around us,
    *Fall out!*

Hunger that knows no rest,
    *Eat yourself!*

You monsters
that come flickering out of your bombshelter souls
to strike at the life we try and make
in spite of you:
>*May you become the bad dreams*
>*you push on us and our children*
>*and never wake!*

Meantime: KEEP OUT OF THESE WOODS.

You're scaring my friends.

# Coyote at the Movies

We've all seen it before—Weyerhaeuser, Georgia Pacific, Simpson Timber, Crown Z.—the same forestry promo film, rundown of the industry from forest tree to suburb box; but when Coyote got hold of the lost film can and took a look at the end of the reel, *he* knew immediately how to run it, and invited all his friends.

So—the finished tract houses and tormented lawns and shrubs, that so upset and displaced all the animals there, became the beginning.

"Here we are," said Coyote, and all agreed.

But suddenly there appeared a whole crew of human workers who carefully and quickly began taking the houses down—shingle by board by window by door, and loaded the pieces into large flat trucks. In a flash the trucks had delivered the lumber to a great lodge Coyote told them was the Lodge of Many Healing Wheels, told them he'd been there himself, at night, and seen it all. Inside, the great wheels, with teeth sharper than Beaver's, spin all the boards back into logs again. No one had ever seen anything like this. (Even Coyote was taken aback at the sight.) And in awe they watched the logs be carried by huge machines larger than elephants and loaded onto long trucks which—driving backward so the trees could steer them to exactly where they wanted to be—carried them through many small towns far into the mountains on special roads built just for them. It was such a wonderful sight even the old man himself had to smile. All those old trees going back home.

Once there, there were huge towers as high as a Douglas-fir, that carefully lowered the logs down to just their precise spots on the hillside. The squirrels were beside themselves! But who are these blue-shirted workmen who wait in the brush? Coyote says they are shamen who possess magic wands of smoke. And if everyone watched closely, they would see them placing all the limbs and branches back onto the broken trees. Amazing! They were even joining and healing the cut trunks back together! Everyone agreed these must be powerful priests (and marveled at the special herbs they kept in small tins in their pockets and kept adding to endlessly from behind their lips).

"They all work for me," Coyote said, but no one was listening. Instead, they were watching the shamen wave their wands over the stumps, and the trees would leap into the air amid great clouds of needles and dust and noise.—Everyone ducked, and when they looked again, the trees sat majestically back on their stumps, unscratched!

Now there were such great cheers from the crowd that Rabbit had to place his forepaws into his ears, and Mole hurriedly dug his way underground. Coyote, he decided right then and there that was just the way he was going to work things. And that he was going to start the very next day, "Even if it takes a while," he thought out loud. "Yes, even if it takes a good long time."

## Two Puddle Sutra

Following the trail back
last night, moonless,
        without shadow,
I stumbled on a small
        just-formed pool—
     a few stars held in its depths—
and stopped short.

Something
inside me leapt back,
afraid to fall into the endlessness there.

It was as if the ground we walk on is ground
    and not ground, too.
Sometimes a footbridge strung tenuous
       across the mind.
     Beneath it the emptiness widens
       into its pale stars.

As if some night, on some too-familiar path,
suddenly, it all falls through
        —like that!
And held there:
   the breath slowly returning,
     when all the while
     all I ever really had to do
      was stoop down,
      drink a little,
       be on my way.

# Winter Song in the Foothills

On the coldest nights
when the scattered chips
of winter stars
light the valley with frost,
the frozen lakes will sometimes
sing to themselves.

Their song
echoes through the snowforest hills
and still dense midnight air
like a great kettledrum
rumbling deep and hollow
in the belly of earth.

Plates of ice shift and settle
against their banks of pasture
and wood,
while this strange and restless music
drifts past the frosty ears
of cows, owls
tucked in the hollows of night,
the gentle sleeping bears,

and carries up the hillside creeks
to startle us from sleep
—no song like we ever heard before—
and rock the house softly
on its moorings of ashes and dust.

# Moonrabbit

The Moonrabbit
follows his forepaws out
from dappled shadow to light.
One eye
holds the moon's cold lamp,
the other is one with the night.

The moon herself
is in eclipse,
half dark with the earth, half true.
And her creatures
both those who hunt and who—
lured by the shimmering play of blue

and broken light—are hunted,
fetch their way
through a gate of white dew.
Many small eyes
wink out of the night
but those who approach us are few.

And fewer still
who deign to come
now when the cups of sake are done.
But Moonrabbit's ears
lift past a sleeve
as he peers over all who sleep, and one

or a few, still awake
in their coats, high
above towns in the glimmering night.
In secret, Moonrabbit
sifts through their dreams and
sets the course of their days aright.

*(Lunar eclipse viewing, Mount Zion)*

# Moon, Horses, and Groundfog

A corner of dream opened
into night—soft ring
of the bell mare, close
to the open shelter where I slept.

A low fog had moved up from the river,
and the dark shapes of horses grazed
knee-deep in silvery light.

In the hazy reach between sleep
and waking,
I was among them, tasting the fog
that was our ground. It was cool,

and smelled of leafmulch,
of dampened ash,
and the slow breath of a glacier.

The moon stood still in a spruce tree,
and the sound of the river
moved away over polished stones.

I was midpoint on a journey
I had forgotten I'd begun,
and the dust of winter stars
covered the empty shoes beside me.

# [ 11 ]
## GEESE AND REEDS

# "Geese and Reeds"

Yüan Dynasty,
Artist unknown

The air hangs thick
and a few
    autumn reeds
    bend at the shore of a river.

The geese
are wet from the long flight.

One rests,
while two
    reach at the water's edge,
calling
to others maybe lost in fog.

Washed-ink lines fade
    into old paper.

Their call is a window
opening into early winter,
a poem
    gleaned once on a journey,

the rain just turning to snow.

# As a Heron Unsettles
# a Shallow Pool

for Mary

At times
when the too-many threads
of our speech become knots,
and words
fall back on us unsaid;

when I go brooding across wet fields
to the river, and you
in the kitchen alone.

When the earth itself is burdened,
as if the sky
or the weight of the sky
were suddenly too much for her—
the rain-drenched maples bent low
               and crossed,
words too quickly cast.

A stillness
heavy as snow.

Then, as a heron unsettles a shallow pool,
as it lifts blue wings
and leaps
slowly into the downstream wind,

the weight of love finds its own wings,
unfolded as slowly, one
to each.

And as a pale band of sky opens
at dusk,
so the heart will open.
The smoothly rippled flow
—river of our days—
unsettling
        in a litany of light.

# Morning of Birds

for Mary

You said *"Look . . . "*
Past the door, four swans
were breasting the still morning mist;
frost along the sedge
      and lake-edge grasses,
   the thinnest lens of ice.

And atop a leaning spruce
an eagle, glowing faintly
    in the early light.

The swans utter soft
muted calls
almost like the calls of geese:
whistlers.
While out from the shadowed reeds,
two, and three more
—one the darker gray of the young—
echoing back
the deep wintry call.

It is before the first sun.
Wood ducks feed in the marshgrass;
small ripples
move soundlessly out
      over luminescent water.

*"... a morning of birds."*

Your words,
and the day loosening itself
out of the intricate blossoms of frost.

# Feather

### for Robert Sund

Coming upon the creek where it fanned down the beach still early in the day, we stopped to drink and rest. The dawn clouds had blown clear and most of the shorebirds were off feeding in the morning tide. One small bird, a cliff swallow, stayed and, swooping close to us, snatched a feather from the sand without breaking flight. With it she shot up on the inshore wind until she hovered almost motionless, then, letting it drop, wheeled a wide sweeping arc some fifty yards up the beach, and turning and falling back into the wind—a slight quiver of the tailfeathers guiding—swept back full spread on the downdraft, and caught the drifting, wind-spun feather just as it would touch the ground.

We sit wrapped as she turns a hundred swirls and faults, tumbling skyward and again lets the feather fall. The two a single motion, a rhythm of wind, a dance over the waves' dance, until for no reason, the swallow glints away and the feather drifts calmly into the wood.

The bird hardly a season old, yet turning such grace with a feather. I thought of myself stumbling days over words, trying to lift one line off the ground.... And the flight was simply the joy of the bird; we two just happened to be there in time. And in time we rose and hiked to town; got there late and missed our ride. But this: all the while something inside us circled and lifted against our skin, seemed to flow out of and into us like breath. A something, becoming more than ourselves, and spun, humming all around us.

# One for the Dipper

*(Cinclus mexicánus)*

To be as sure
& light-footed among rapids
as the dipper:

slate-gray puff
of feather & song
twiglike yellow feet

*dip, dip,* on a sudsing rock
cheeps off upstream
no higher than spray...

one yesterday—
drinking delicate little
beakfuls

from a boulder
mid-Dungeness
wild with three weeks' rain.

# Ka'houk

Dawn
stirs the mists
once

over the ancient lake.

She lifts her head just
long enough to see,

settles back against me.

Treeshapes
fold into the fog;

a pintail circles her dream.

We have been asleep
for a hundred years

and all the old names
have crept back

like moss.

*(Ozette Lake)*

# *Ohalet*

A late sun
follows down river;
bands of shadow
climb the long columns of trees.

Kneeling among roots
of a whiskery spruce,
brushing out her hair
        silver
    in the last sunlight,

a faint ripple of wind:

*Ohalet.*

"Quickly moving one."

The farther I go
the deeper...
      and a doe
steps lightly into us.

*(Hoh River)*

# Mount Mystery

for C.

Because you stopped
midway down the snowgully
from Gunsight Pass
to mend my torn packstrap,

and later, pushing up through
slide alder and brush
in the full press of midday heat,
I got antsy when you slipped
into a nap, resting on steep talus,
and woke you up;

I want this poem to go back
and do what I
didn't have the grace to do:
lay its thin shirt over your shoulders,
whisper *we'll be there*

into your sleep,
and watch the first shadows
begin to cool the deep jade of valleys
and thickets we'd come through,
the loose cobble beneath the mystery
that surrounds us.

# The Saw-whet's Song

Alone, dusk
and the saw-whet's whistle.

The same time of year,
I thought, that we followed
—waist-deep in marshgrass & fern—
that same ambient song.

Owl spirit.
Cold sentient heart
of the hollows. At dark
we turned back
toward the lamp in the window.

A search as vague,
illusive as the years we spent
caught in a sometimes song
in the deepening shadows,

that small feathered life
we never found.

# Lake La Crosse

Sometimes the mountains
are bitter medicine.
Sundown and miles from camp.

I once wrote a poem—winter
on the coast—sitting alone
with the women I'd driven away.

Now the same barren ridges and draws
the mosquito hosts, the old
fields of snow in the shadows.

A broken ridgetop
like an impossible traverse
back to you, that I couldn't do.

Bitter, sometimes, lost
and aching in their loveliness.

# Morning

1

Up fighting half the night
and the cold quiet hours
awake.

The space between the owl's
hoot
opens mouse-eyed
wide.

Morning is an old woman
carrying a wheel
through a field of flowers.

2

And morning lies in mist
over the fields,
day lifts wisps of smoke
like reeds
from an empty lake.

3

We say
nothing
or next to nothing.

The sky through the leaves
in two teacups
grows cold.

# Evening

Walking the tracks
between the shacks of two old friends:
one just gone to the city,
the other unseen for months.

A high overcast
lifts back past the mountains
and the low sun lulls the bay
slate blue.

A day the dreams
turn back in their old shoes,
and evening becomes again
evening.

Hermit thrush
echoes over the sound of trucks,
and the worn and rusted tracks
can't measure the distance.

# Indian Island

for Steve Johnson

Upstairs, along the far wall
of the loft,
past the still lifes and studies,
your painting shares the corner
with a window to the rainy night.

A blown tuft of summer grass,
a cloudless sky,
and underneath the ground, seen
as if in X-ray,
a tier of bombs stacked
in harsh yellow glare.

This evening no one is near it.

Across the bay, cut into the shore
of a small wooded island,
the half-built landing dock
—which will carry
the most destructive weapons on earth—
waits
in chill winter rain.

I can't tell
if the painted frame of darkness
that fades and bleeds to a band of light
on the horizon
represents a sunset or dawn.

I want to think dawn, but the colors
are lit with a beauty that comes
only with endings.
The beauty of embers or leaves,
ranges of stone worn to grassland,
the roll of continents asleep
beneath a burning sea.

# The Ride Home
### for Jay Sisson

Summer leans its borrowed leaves
toward solstice—a year now
since the morning you left
to finish yarding a cut over on Cabin Creek,
and didn't come back.

A month's overcast has just lifted
and the high meadows are opening again.
Creeks all noisy and ice-green in sunlight,
goldenrod and thistle in the uncut hay:
the time of year you'd lead the Clydesdales
from Leland Valley, up past the cabin
and down to fresh pasture on the other side.

I still see the great hoofprints at the crossings,
their small wells filled with night,
and an old shirt you left on a peg by the door
hung there most of a year.

Too many things
we don't let go to each other,
washing down the taste of exhaust and sawdust,
Quilcene paydays after work. Jay,
you were too young and quick-footed
to have to pay so dearly for the ways
of this mean and greedy land.

Rain to willowbloom, ashes to grass;
but yours is the always joy
of having the old truck running good,
and filled with a load of freshly poached cedar,
and a bottle of Jim Beam for the long ride home
by dark.

# Another Stormed-in Day
# on the Mountain

(after Li Po)

Days like this
I would
Write a poem for you
Full of clouds and loneliness.
But today
You're here with me,
We can talk quietly
Beneath the rattling rain.

Along the east ridge of
Bear Mountain,
The first dusting of snow.
And beneath the goosedown cover
Your body
Still brown with summer.

Let the seasons
Sweep past as they may,
Day by day
Even the smallest creeks
Find their way home.

# The Queets

We worked through dinner
on a windfall spruce above Pelton Creek,
a tree thick as we were tall.
Wedging our cuts, edging peevee & shim,
wheel after slow-turning wheel
to near dark.
Smoothed out the trail tread,
packed our tools and started back
seven miles downriver to camp.

Past Bob Creek the last light
was loosening itself from the grass,
falling from the moss shoulders
of maple and alder.
A doe and her yearling browsed
the far riverbank, and somewhere nearby
a flicker tapped randomly.
The river
carried with it its own light,
and coursed slowly through the late summer bottom.

The tools lay in a pile
where I'd dropped them at the trailside;
my partner hadn't yet caught up.
All I knew
at the worn and frazzled end of that long day
was the last light slipping from us,
the chill air
troughing down dark timbered slopes,
and the lucent voice of the river
telling me it no longer mattered.

# [III]
## TUNDRA SONGS

# Tundra Song

The cairn people
range wide
over this low ebbing land

from hummock top to distant
hummock,
tracing the wind's shiftless way,
they

are the sole inhabitants
among drifters & birds;
they plant their stone feet
deep in it

—coarse, dry fleck of lichen,
tundra rose
adrift in matted heather—

briefly, between the snows,
they make one feel
at home, almost,
alone

in the wide & quiet emptiness
of the days.

# Song to the Northern Lights

Aurora, goddess
whose hair is diamond,
"lights of the northern wind."

From a midnight peak up the Sitkum:
    luminous
        shifting
            prolix ... almost liquid
and clean as cut ice.

In the high still emptiness
where the sun's fingers play
          with the dark,
altering gasses ...

or ancient Eskimo spirits
lifting colored lamps
to guide the dead across.

    Shimmering brightness
    from some other place,
    light
    at the heart of all things—

"like looking through
    or out of a jewel,"

or black Raven's eye
as he spans the black sky
      over the chasm.

# Dusk

Five lean stalks of grass
shiver
on the windy bar;

night cools the parched
autumn tundra,
gathers mists from an open palm.

There's a homelessness leads one
to sleep where he may,
a loneliness
brings one to a cricket's call
at dusk.

High, frayed wisp of geese
forever coming apart yet
holding their pattern
east;

that same
subtle web of thought
buried somewhere in us—

flapping
willy-nilly across the empty dome.

# The River I

Along the south bank of the McKinley,
close to dark:
the fresh tracks of what look to be
    a young caribou,
  and following, over them,
      the larger track of wolf.

Clouds deepen the mountain night;
a hawk owl circles the stones.

I build a cairn to mark our crossing.
It stands
like a man who has waited too long for something.

By morning
only the river is left singing.

# The River II

Who live here speak footfall and wind.
Caribou, belly-deep in willow,
lifts his antlers and drifts away.
Ptarmigan flutter tails in fright.

Grizzly has led her children up a ravine:
she rests now, almost sleeping.
The tips of her fur shine with icelight.

Downriver, Raven draws circles
around a story his uncle left unfinished.
Already the small hoofed feet are dancing
far over the tundra.

# Frost

August blueberries, arctic cranberries,
gathered in a wooden bowl
(whole bushes uprooted where the bears
    have been, branches sucked to the pith).
Already in the low carpet of tundra
a slight shift in color:
deep greens fading some,
faint tinges of red among the huckleberry
                and fireweed,
and the lowest leaves of the dwarf willow
      yellowing
   like the pages of an old book
      left out too long in a shed
      unread:

   this from a single frost.

# McGonagall Pass

Back and forth through
        thick mountain fog,
    through arctic summer rain:

the lost cries of snow geese
        miles
    from any lake.

# Letter from the Interior

Hail rattles the thin tent walls
of our lives,
winds from canyons we barely know.

If I reach now
out through the ice and distance,
reach past the ranges of fear.

Cupped in your hands
a wild bird's egg,
fern rustles around you like wings;

and when you turn
the summer sky of your eyes
to me,

and the footholds soften
in the old snow...

# Radovin

Dying embers, Chitistone wind,
waiting out the weather
in an old miner's shack:
autumn mountain rain.

Across the creek,
long switchback up the cliffside,
packing it all on your back; bit
and powder charge, spring to fall,
every day a little deeper
into the glinting memories of earth.

By candlelight,
the rough-hewn walls and thin
plank shelves are still littered
with bank notices, forms
from the Bureau of Mines—tattered
and mouse-nibbled: Glacier Creek
via Cordova, 1964.

Stew simmers in your old pot,
the blackened iron stove.
I almost expect you to duck in
out of the rain,
Radovin,
park your lonely ghostly bones down
on a bench,
spit against the stove.

One by one
the empty bucket loads
roll past on the washed-out road.

Rainy mornings, cross-legged,
deeper into the bottomless mind—

No strike, no hidden vein,
just you and me, ghost, and the rain
over the slant tarpaper roof.
Was it
somewhere in the pick and shovel-bending
work of it
came the prize?

Or late afternoon at the tunnel-mouth,
shadows playing against high canyon walls,
an eagle
dropping from the snowy light.

# At the Foot of Denali

At the edge of a storm
a few drops scatter over broken talus,
deepen the palm-smooth texture of shale:
    thin bands of rust, delicate
           trace of lichen—
  so slightly,
and the wind blows it dry.

Above us the ice, blue
against a dark motionless sky.
A tumult stream buries itself,
its song
      a long steady windlike thing
lost beneath the glacier's edge.

In the early light
small patches of moss weave footholds;
        stonecrop
    wedged among banks of gravel
saxifrage:
some small nameless insect
  fluorescent-winged at its blossoms.

The birds and mammals have yet to be born,
salmon to try these ice-bound streams.
The trees have long ago turned back.

And we come
slow and bedraggled, strung
together like beads on a thread.
　　Long heaps of shattered rock,
　　dark walls lifting into clouds,
　　　　snow-streaked, wind-worn . . .

Come from the war dance on terrazzo floors,
come from the arms of strangers,
Cold one; come
as though this northern reach of wind and snow
were somehow
all that's left for earth.

As though this train of ice, slow
and barren miles
out to the plain where life begins,
were the first river.

And far down a doorstep valley
a people live in peace.

# [IV]
## LAST YEAR'S POVERTY

# Last Year's Poverty

for Mike O'Connor

Last year's poverty was truly enough poverty,
but this year's poverty is poverty indeed.
—*Hsiang-yen*


The first winter snow
dusts our boots across the stubble field
              (squeak of fencepost)
    to the chicken house.

Must've been a hundred of 'em in there
blinking, squawky in the weird light:
the wild, the exotic, and the plain.

              (Not to mention the five
              extra roosters I dumped
              on you last summer...)

They hop down from their perches,
sleepily begin their various chicken dances
                over the dusty straw—
while you scour all the nests
for supper.

At last
you find one egg.

        "Not a bad life,"
                —cupping it like a jewel, out
into the frost-thinned moonlight—
        "no,
        fella could do worse,
                they tell me."

61

# The Day After Reagan Sweeps the Country Quigley and I Hike into Cedar Flat Scrounging for Salvage Cedar in Hopes of Making Ends Meet

"The key to our nation's prosperity lies in economic growth
and full employment . . . through new opportunities for labor
and business to produce together."
—*Ronald R.*

While the storm
held and built past the ridges,
we combed the draws
upstream and back,
Howe Creek, Cedar Creek, moss

so thick on the deadfall
we sunk in it,
upended stumps in the swamps
long since picked clean;
a half-century's benign neglect
and not one solid log.

Found an old salvage show
high on the ridge, yarded
with donkey and sled.
The culls were reworked
just last summer: spolt
left the length of vanished logs.

By mid-afternoon the winds were up,
the first darts of a coming rain.
Already there's the look
of a hard winter
and he hasn't assumed office yet!

We sit, tired, on the old logroad,
take a last look at the map.
State and federal and corporate
ownerships scattered
multicolored over the land.
We wonder who it was
decided all this anyway,
and how many of those old stumps
ever had a vote.

# After Losing the Bid on a Season's Treeplanting to an Out-of-Work Fisherman, We Take a Hike Up Barnes Creek and Reflect on the Nature of the Times

for Kevin & Finn

In the frozen shade of an old forest
we cut through stiff winter brush, and climb
to the base of the oldest tree we can find.

Its deeply furled bark is charred
by centuries of fires, and looks almost
rocklike beneath pale gray-green lichens.

All the out-of-work treeplanters in two counties
stacked up on each other's backs (which
isn't far from the truth)
couldn't match its height.

> "It's good to be around someone
> who's lived through harder times than these."

Out along 101, no log trucks or tourists,
but Barnes Creek moving its quiet stones,
building its delta incrementally into the lake,

like a ghost crew of Chinese coolies,
or an old tired CCC gang
who never got the news about Roosevelt.

# Gamble

He cleared a place on the dusty seat
And started north toward the bridge.

"...Leland? Sure, I know that country.
Used to pack in up Skaar Pass way.
Hunt bobcat. Was cat all through there
one time, cougar, fox, why...
I give it up though. I just...
well, I give it up."

The foothills along the far shore
Drift deeper into cloud,
Toandos, South Point, afloat.
Rain down the Canal held there.

"Got five acres over there.
Bought it from Pope. Got themselves
a fair piece, they do.
That mill up Gamble's the oldest
in the country. Still operating."

He leaned toward the window, spat.

"Yes, I work for them. My father, too.
Started when he was ten—that was
before the child labor laws.
Come out here with his mom, two brothers.
She took tubercular. Died.
Him 'n' his brothers went to work
pullin' slab.

"Retired when he was sixty-five.
But y'know, two months later
he gets a stroke. Died
just after that."

His eyes
Climbed a wooded hill
Faltered, and came to rest on the still
Gray-green waters
Darkening in the shadows of second growth.

"Yeah,
oldest sawmill in the damn country."

# I Consider Once More the Walls

Thunder rumbles up the canyon
and cold rain blows in from Canada.
Another day hangs in mists through the trees.
Chickadees sing but once.

With nine miles of wet clothes
for a pillow,
I consider once more the walls of the tent,
the lost joys of hibernation, going
back to school, finding a job...

My lover has tunneled down
into her sleeping bag and won't come out.
Near dark
a tiny tree frog hops up beneath the rain fly
and shudders.

# Old Town

Poking through the second-hand
junk store piles of pants—
one good pair: baggy, hard wool, stained a bit.
Downstairs the old guys are talking Reno,
"Lake Tye-hoe..."
Past Bellingham Bay clouds are lifting,
log rafts rustle and nudge in the smoke.

A dollar fifty-nine cents.

I could go borrow the difference
or try to talk the guy down to a buck.
Eight years ago, bought a good pair here
for fifty cents; but times change.
The great wheels of the world
spin wildly past the used-pants set.
Most everybody else for that matter.

"Yeah, Lake Tye-hoe;
that place is the *dickens!*"

# Out of Work, Walking the Quilcene River After an Early Snow

The brush alder along the abandoned trail
(whose limbs I used to push through arms first)
have closed above me in a lattice of snow.

Snow-softened foothills, blue panes of sky.
Another winter out of work
and the river cranky in its rocky bed.

I think of the poet O Cen-wen,
and the haywire schemes he'd try
to skinny by on.
                    The empty truck
is parked in the snow,
and the fresh tracks of all our protégés—
coyote, rabbit, bobcat, deer—
cross and tangle up with mine:
                    each
    contained in its own singular way
    of getting (or not getting) through
            these lean and awkward times.

The old Buddhas of Bark Shanty
drape snow-heavy limbs over the river,
while beneath them
the charred stones of hunters' fires
have become small fonts of whiteness.

I sit by one
and consider the way of the mouse
who leaves his small three-track, tail-foot
    trail over the new snow
        and always moves in circles;

        or blackbear
who possesses the deep sagacity
to hole up in a stump and doze
till spring spreads her lush green paycheck
    over the cold and stony world.

# From the City
A poem for the
Bonneville Power Administration

Hiking home the back way
hungover, with a pack full of books.
Low clouds dredge the north;
a sparse October rain hangs
in the even ranks of second growth.
Slowly, up the muddy spur
where giant steel skeletons
march over the cropped hills
like aberrant soldiers.
The lost song of the Columbia
buzzing aimless
through wires no bird sings from.

# [ V ]
## THE STONE OWL

# Roads

All through dinner
the incessant talk of blowing away elk,
deer, goat, antelope . . .
Scope, bore, and grains to the load—I let
the screen door bump shut on it.

In the cooling rainforest dusk,
the soft-lit grass of an alder bottom draws me
out to a band of willows
                    by the river.

I'm stopped
by the startled jump and stare of a young elk—
a three-point bull—his head
and newly polished horns alert, upright
            and facing me.
To calm him, I tell who I am,
what I'm up to,
        soft-voiced and even,
                moving slowly toward the river.

He turns back to his browse
of willow leaves and bark, but
checks on me every now and again,
while I pretend to munch some alder
        (so as not to seem too odd)
and talk of this & that.

*"Be careful . . . "* at last, *"for god sake!"*

And because his antlers gleam
        like polished amber,
a small prayer
to make it through the fall hunt,
and long walk back through darkening woods
to the bunkhouse;

from these wild, strange, and unchanging friends
in the brush
to those other friends I live and work with,
who kill them.

# Three Poems for Deer

1

Last spring, on a bank just up the creek,
I found the smoothed and fur-dusted bed
of a deer.
Nested beneath low boughs,
brush browsed back, the smell was still fresh.
But so close, I thought,
within sight of the cabin.

It had been a harsh season.
Many deer were wintering
down close to the valley bottoms and farms.
Dawns, you would see them
browsing a far corner of pasture,
kneading up the snow.

Here, far enough in from the dogs,
there was cover, fresh water...
And the nights I sat at my desk unknowing,
and the lamplight
found its way through the frost-lit trees,
what, if anything, did it mean to her
—nipping at her winter coat
to make a bed for the fawns,
sharing our water for a time.

2

Traversing into Boston Basin from Eldorado Peak,
nearly a mile above the North Fork of the Cascade,
a day so hot and thick with flies
we cursed it.
At a deep, steep-sided gorge—
Bob saw him first—a great old buck
asleep, we thought, by the creek side.
Once across though, and from sixty feet above,
we could see he was bloated, unable to move,
and had obviously come here
—where a slight wind kept down the flies
and there was water enough—
to die.

On the hottest day of the year
he had climbed past the last subalpine trees,
this remote basin, to be left alone with death.
Seeing this, and that our presence
caused him distress, I left
feeling as though I had committed an unforgivable act.

A prayer for his spirit, and silence
as we worked down through the rocks and thick
summer meadows, stream-ribboned cliffs,
and the first thin reaches of forest—
the cold rending beauty of a land
empty of sentiment or promise.

3

Three mornings now, fresh tracks
in the snow where the deer's trail
crosses mine.
Just a little earlier than me, I can tell.
And like me they stop
and look at those *other* tracks—
their loitering prints almost show
the large ears leaning forward as they sniff.

A browsed cedar shrub, freshly nipped salal.
Where do they go and why such regular hours?
I'm sure we wonder about each other
every morning, here where the trails cross,
mingle, and slip singularly past
into the same world.

# A Poet's Job

In the early
          spring morning frost,
two deer
browse the huckleberry shoots
from Crown Zellerbach's holding
    over into Scott Paper.

A poet's job is a tricky one.

# A Transmission:
# Fall in the Wind Rivers

High over the easy roll of sagebrush desert,
Wyoming cattle flat, late in season,
Mexicans are herding sheep
down from the upper meadows.
Afternoon, their pack train traces the far
edge of the lake, and now, when the wind ebbs,
a soft baying
clambers over the still water.

A river of small shapes the color of boulders
works its way among the trees
and smooth rock ledges,
sheep dogs yap at its banks, and herdsmen
ride easy in thick woolen coats, rifles
like crooks at their knees.

By evening the meadows south of the lake are
abloom with them.

Snowclouds lean
past the dull gray peaks of the divide;
the wind lifts out of Utah.
We bank our fire against a crop of granite,
sit close with our small cups of steam.
A hundred summers they've pastured here,
and winters the freight cars east.

I thought of my grandfather; how his talk,
those last days, would shift
and weave through a number of European tongues,
and the fading eyes would fill with light.
    "He's talking about the mountains
    where he used to pasture sheep
    in the old country."
The old man who shared his room would
nod and chuckle. And I
listened to the music of his words, not knowing
then, what it was turned the stern old patriarch
to a child.

Midnight, a cold dusting of snow,
and morning to follow the fresh tracks of winter.
Descend from the high country and pack the truck,
trace the slowing rivers west.
Already late enough in season, and an older
and harder worked voice is coaxing me
to a month, maybe two months' more work
in the mountains
of a different coast, before the snows.

# Gatha for the
# Buddha at Marymere

Stopped—midst a scramble
between two jobs—
    just off the lip of Lake Crescent.

A cold wind from the Strait
buoyed clouds over whitecaps,
and scattered small patches of light
across the damp forest floor
    like coins tossed to a supplicant.
Winter wrens flit through mossy roots,
while a hundred feet up, all the trees
        frozen in new snow.

Pulled down my hat,
switched up the narrow ravine-side trail
and old cedar rail
        to the falls.
A sheer rock shelf
where the creek, for a moment,
      loses itself;
drops
    freely through the canyon updraft
    —spray dancing &
        spinning off—
then
becomes creek again.

Above, the mountain climbs onward
about its business,
but here
it's as though something
breaks away from contour and course,
becomes, for a moment,
            its own boundless element.

On the smooth stone face around it,
        a great Buddha-halo
            of moss.

And the maidenhair fern
        clings to the cliff edge,
    and shadows deepen across the pool,
        and the trail bows to a stop.

# The Crows

The Pacific flings its rain
in sheets against the bent and wooded shore,
flings it with a vengeance,
while a rasty batch of crows
holds safe in a spruce on the headland.

With cocked beaks and a rasp
of a laugh,
they watch this poor naked bird
enter the chaos of the river.

The only two-legged soul in miles,
what brings him—awobble—
     mid-stream midst the roll of boulders,
the whitecaps poised at his wrist?

The crows, clearly amused, hop from limb to limb
as the pack, hoisted
too high out of the current,
         topples,
    footing slips loose.
       A sudden lurch, curse, splash
     & stumble to the shallows lands him
breathless and blue on the far rocks.

The crows
now raucous—flapping a storm
in their storm-battered tree—
are the clear notes
of all my erstwhile plans
      gone wrong—
of what sees me through
    in worry and in song.

*(Fording the Ozette River, Christmas, 1980)*

# Caitlin and the Bear

My daughter had nearly passed the tree
by the time I noticed it: a mossy cedar
with the buttressed swell of its base
stripped clean to bright sapwood;
shreds of ripped bark and woodchips
scattered over the trail like leaves.

"Caitlin," I called, "Who ate that?"
She stopped and her gaze climbed
to the claw-torn edge of bark
higher than me. And she:
"Somebody big."

We felt the wiggly tracks
of beetle larvae,
powder-filled furrows in the orange wood,
and the claw marks raked across them.

"Somebody," I said,
"must have been awfully hungry."
And Caitlin, as if suddenly
looking up at one across the dinner table,
sang out, "A *bear!*"
And then, just as quickly, "Where is it?"

So we looked,
through ferns, out past the tall columns
of trees, behind us ...
"He must have wandered off," I said;
then, catching her mother's quick glance, added
"a few weeks ago."

We should have known that later
she would find him,
a shadowy figure among the ferns
that looked to us like a stump.
But we all kept right on walking anyway,
just in case.

# The Skagit Stone Owl

1
The smooth-washed riverstone
still shows through:
carved roundness
of shoulders and wings,
the curved bowl of stomach.

Your head
leans to the side and slightly
downward,
as from the height of a low branch.

As if to utter a name.
You who were messenger of death,
whose eyes of timeless
mineral vision see through
the small lives and deaths
of the world
to the singular life that holds them.

A century ago
a young Skagit man, journeying
far from his village,
heard your voice.
Late, when the burden of hope
had left him.

Returning downriver afoot,
he chose
the one among thousands of perfect
riverstones.

And the song you had given him
grew strange and beautiful
wings
which opened the sealed dome of night.


2
Cupped in the smooth
porous bowl of your stomach
were herbs mixed with oolichan oil,
potions to heal
or aid one through his passage.

Now you cradle only
the old emptiness,
Owl,
and a glint of museum light
not at all like the moon.

I can't tell what it is in you
holds me
silent at the glass case
where the carved dreams and dances
of a life so different from mine
keep their silences.

Only, that when I turn
to go, I'm taken by a feeling:
lightness in the limbs,
a fullness inside my chest—

And a sudden glimmer
of vision:
as though death were merely
the night,
and I the eyes and wings of Owl.
To fall from the self
and fly through.

Some undreamed shape
wondrous and new,
in the first cool mists of dawn.

# Winter Solstice Eve
# Descending Graywolf Valley

Snow on the upper slopes
has given way to rain along the river.
High storm clouds roll north
while a light bank of cloud moves
mistlike up valley, west.

Adrift in the shallow band of clearing,
spur ridges climb briefly
to nowhere;
their combtooth treetops sift the fog,
and a fine rain
falls on slant floors of moss and lichen,
      wetting the chestnut backs of deer,
        fretting the winter wren home.

Along a narrow rocky bar,
an eagle takes his winter meal of spawned salmon.
His tail and head feathers
show luminous in the gray-turquoise light
of the river at dusk.

As I approach
he lifts his wings slowly into the dark trees.

Sutherland Creek, Twin Creek, flat
bouldery terrace where the river
leans and cuts at its bank, and the trees lean.
Others, behind them, stand
as they have stood at the turn of countless years
—rain and snow—who know

the vanished wolves' call
and the pull of toppling storm winds
in their limbs,

and to whom these turns
of the year must come as days,
and the seasonal pulse of the river
like the chords of a song,
        never undone:

    *Cloud-mover,*
    *Salmon-giver,*
    *Stones all gone to sand*
        *at your feet.*

## About the Author

Tim McNulty is a poet, conservationist, and nature writer who lives with his family in the northern foothill country of Washington State's Olympic Peninsula. He is the author of five books of poetry and seven books of natural history, including an award-winning series of books on national parks, co-authored with photographer Pat O'Hara. His poems have been published widely in the U.S. and Canada, and his nature writings have been translated into German and Japanese. McNulty's articles on natural history and conservation issues have appeared in numerous magazines and journals, and he remains active in Northwest environmental issues.

Design by Nick Gregoric.

Text set in ITC Century Book with Engravers Bold Face No. 9
using the KI/Composer and Linotronic 202N.
Typeset by Blue Fescue Typography and Design,
Seattle, Washington.

Broken Moon Press books are printed on
acid-free, recycled paper exclusively by
Malloy Lithographing, Inc.,
5411 Jackson Road,
Ann Arbor, Michigan 48106.